AND YOU WONDER WHY...

———————

By: SHEMARYAH MANNIE

And You Wonder Why
Copyright © 2020 by Shemaryah Mannie

All rights reserved. Printed in the U.S.A.
No part of this book may be reproduced in whole or any partial form, transmitted in any form, electronic or mechanical, including photocopying and recording, or by any information storage or retrieval system, or by any means without written permission from the author.

ISBN 978-1-7358270-0-1

Published By: Niyah Publishing Company
niyahpublishing@yahoo.com

Attention: A Face Without Shame
P.O. Box 378583
Chicago, IL 60637 www.afacewithoutshame@yahoo.com
shemaryahmannie@yahoo.com

Dedication

This book is dedicated to my children Jeremiyah and Zakariyah who are the reason for this production. A special dedication to my baby Amariyah for helping me to strengthen and redefine myself through her presence. I am grateful to my eldest daughter for demonstrating patience, remaining supportive, and loving, when those were all needed. To my family, thank you for your support, advice, and love. A special thanks to a great man who has been by my side, encouraging me into greatness; forever my friend, Billy Brown. Also, without the love, strength, patience, and protection from the Most-High, writing this book would not be possible. Thank you all for your contributions, I am sincerely grateful and blessed!

Table of Contents

Dedication..3

Contents..4

Introduction 5

Chapter 1 .... The Exposure of My Youth....................8

Chapter 2 ....The Duplicated Anger........................14

Chapter 3 .... The Hurt I Feel....................................20

Chapter 4 .... Learning to Let Go..............................26

Chapter 5 .... A Promise to Myself...........................32

Introduction

This book was essential as it was lived through the lenses of two vulnerable children who suffered internally due to their father not being a part of their growth and development. The children unfortunately, witnessed abuse beginning in infancy into adolescence. These two children struggled to live in a world where they felt like outcasts. No one seemed to understand them; their mother was no saint, still, she never walked away from her children. Their mother fought unconditionally to keep them together, but the streets, the system and hell was fighting to take them down. It was extremely difficult to grow up year after year for Ariel and Miciayah to see their father and he not embrace them, the way they needed. The hurt they carried for years, was taken out on the person closest to them; their mother became the target of displaced anger. The rebellion and furious emotions of feeling unloved and unwanted stagnated in two young souls. Only through perseverance and faith in the Most-High did mom demonstrate the energy, that kept the family afloat and together.

This book was written because the author believed that these children needed to be heard, and their voices do matter. The children wanted to tell their father how his absence affected their life and finally let go to heal. The duo also wanted to use this book as an inspiration to bring families together, in hope that father's step up. Also, to let fatherless children know, it will be ok and they to, will make it through.

When writing this book, the author had in mind, all the hardship she had endured. The failed promises from her children's father. The struggle in search for a husband so that her children would have someone to call dad. Also, the emotional pain of seeing her children suffer for love longed for but not received from their father. Their mother was giving them all of her love and affection. But she had to realize that it was not about her, it was about them and she could only empathize with her children because she did not know their pain. The hopes of writing this book is to encourage fathers to be involved in their children's life because it's not too late to mend a broken heart. Also, for men that meet women who have children and want to be a part of a family, don't be discouraged from giving your love, wisdom, and support to recreate a traditional or blended family. We all need each other if not today, there will be a day that you reach for a hand. Will you have someone to reach for? Or will your karma leave you reaching?

Chapter 1

The Exposure of My Youth

*Ariel Version

Some people say they can't recall their youth. The experiences are blocked from memory, but I remember it all. As a little boy, starting around the age of five years old; I have a lot of memories. Memories that I wish I could erase. Memories that have kept me up at night from sleeping. Kids that go through violence of any kind, become traumatized from a toxic environment. There was a lot of toxicity around me, forcing and pulling me into its cold world. I couldn't do anything about it because I was still new to the world and the people around me had been here for decades long.

I remember seeing and witnessing my father abuse my mother. It was not easy for me as a boy to see my father hit, and bruise my mother, all the time like he did. I did not know what was going on for him to do that, but it happened for years. My mom would cry and try to hide from me, but I would see the results of her face later. My father would act as if nothing happened and blame my mother until she forgave him. They did not know that I was watching, but how could I not hear and see the color lights, loud music and people coming in and out of our apartment all night. Sometimes, the police even came either looking for my father or to put people out of the apartment. I was exposed to so much that it hurts me to talk about it, and I wish it could just be erased from my memory.

There is one memory especially that changed me as a kid. I was seven years old and my father was hurting my mother, he had her down on the ground while hitting her on the living room floor. My mom was crying and screamed my name to help her, telling me to call the police. And as I made an attempt to move and help my mother, my father grabbed me by my shirt and threw me against the wall. That was the moment that hate really built up inside of me.

As the years followed my mother eventually left my father and we did not see him for a while. We stayed in the same neighborhood, but he would bounce from woman to woman and when he did see us sometimes, he acted as if we did not exist. I know I was his third son at the time, but I was still his son, supposedly, his baby boy. I felt hurt and empty many times crying alone and to my mother. I did not understand, why my father did not want me. Why my father never took the time to spend quality time with me, but always was seen with my older brothers. I did nothing wrong except become a product of his seed.

Growing up, my mother taught me so much, but she knew that she could not teach me how to be a man. Therefore, she always tried to keep a cordial relationship with my father. Every time she tried to involve him with raising me, he never stepped up to be a part of my life. I was always disappointed when my father told me he would do something but never did. I missed all the father and son moments, that I longed for. I saw my father on holiday's and family and summer events, but he never made me feel loved. Although, as I got older, he would say I love you son but, I did not feel he ever meant it. I did have a relationship with my siblings and relatives on my father side, so I learned some things from them. One of the things my oldest aunt used to do was implant thoughts in my mind that my mother was the cause of my father's absence. I was a child that did not realize how other people words or actions could influence the development of an individual's character.

Miciayah Version

I don't know if it is sad that I can't recall much of my young moments in life. The moments people cherish and talk about for years to come; like the memories I have seen on television about holidays and fun times with mom and dad. It hurts me because, I can't even clench my eyes to recollect those moments that might have taken place in my life. And if they did, I can't recall them. What I do recall is the number of times that my father would yell, scream, and curse my mother out. I recall seeing my father push my mother at the age of five and seeing my mother on the floor screaming for my brother to call the police. Then my father pushed my brother who was seven years old into the wall in our front room. I witnessed a lot of hurt, pain, separation, and deceit in my youth when I think about my father. I wish things were different growing up, but year after year of living with my father, violence was always present. It followed us no matter where we moved to and somewhere inside of me, it buried itself.

Some of the memories from my youth followed me. All the exposure to so many hurtful experiences I can barely recall. My mother told me it was because it is my repressed memories are stored within my subconscious mind. So, when I behave a certain way, my actions could be related to a traumatic event I experienced. For instance, when I was in fifth grade and there was to be a father's and daughter dance, I would be so angry. I had no father to show up for me and no father figure in my life. Seeing other kids father drop them off to school, play together in the park or a father and daughter sitting at an ice cream shop, would make me upset.

I remember my mother tried so hard to involve him in my life after they separated. She would ask him to participate with buying school clothes and supplies. He only attempted I felt like when he had a new woman and was trying to make her believe that he was a good dad. I did not want much except to be loved and feel loved by my father but, I could never get it the way that I wanted it. I never knew what it felt like to be daddy's little girl. Instead, when my father moved on and had more kids with another woman, I felt like an outcast. I started to go around my stepfamily a little more, but it still was drama.

There were barbeques at my grandmother house and there were always holiday dinners. My mother would always let my brother and me go to my father's mother house for the fourth of July and Thanksgiving. Even though my father had hurt my mother the way he did, she still wanted me to have a dad. My mom told us that she did not want us to ever be mad at her, saying that she kept us away from our father. My mother never took that away from us, no matter how she was trying to heal from the hurt of her past. So, I went to events and shared memories of my father, but it was not enough. Because during those times I always felt like he did not treat me like his daughter.

I will not say that I did not have some fun moments with my father during those times, because I did. But I also had a horrific experience while under my father's care, that when my father did not believe me, it left an internal scar that might not never heal. I was eight years old, and that changed me for the worst. The hurt I did not realize I was carrying continued to bury itself deeper in the core of my soul. My mom has always tried to keep me smiling through all disappointments and sadness, but my anger continually poured onto her. I cannot re-do my youth, but if I could, I definitely would.

Chapter 2

The Duplicated Anger

*Ariel Version

My mother changed my name when I was young. It was a combination of my father's name, but my mother told me that she wanted me to have my own identity. She believed at the time that calling me part of my father's name to address me, would continue the hurt we all carried somewhere inside. My mother stated, she would give me the name of a prophet, so I can be reminded of greatness instead of despair. It was strange even after my name was changed; I had many names. I was the name that my mother originally gave me after birth, by my father's side and on my mother side, I was called my middle name. My mother and people meeting me for the first time were the only ones calling me by my new name.

I was confused, people calling me different names like I was all those different people when I was only one. I was the same young boy that witness pain and hurt in my past. Although, we had moved on and my mother was taking good care of us and she provided well for me, I was still angry. I went to so many diverse schools, in different neighbors in Chicago still it did not change what was going on inside of me. I did not know what was going on inside of me at ten years old, but I expressed it. Every school I went to whether it was a Muslim school, predominantly Hispanic or Black school, I behaved the same way.

At one time in my life, I was much calmer. I believe it was because of my big brother/mentor I was fond of. When

I was eight years old, John, came into my life. My mother signed me up for a program so I could have a male figure to hang out with weekly. I was grateful to have John in my life for the few years I did. Those were wonderful years, I cherish, and I believe when he was in my life, I was trying to overcome my anger and pain for not having my father's presence.

The anger I felt intensified as I got older and continued to visit my grandmother and my father's family. I would hear stories of what my father did for his girlfriend's kids and always felt left out. Especially, when he would tell me he would buy me shoes, but never did. I didn't receive anything, year after year. I was sad and angry about that, but I tried to hide it. I continued to camouflage what I could but if really angered, I would get in rage and use my fist to punch the wall, or people. My mother had to patch up a lot of holes in our apartments during my youth.

As I heard stories from my father's side belittling my mother, I would get furious, but I did not express that to them. I remember being angry at my mother each time I came home and blaming her for my father not having a relationship with me. Everything I would hear my father's family say about my mother, my young mind believed it to be true. I wanted to belong and be accepted by my father and I would make my mother mad and cause her pain, but I had no understanding of what I was doing.

At this time in my life, my mother was single, working and going to school. She often talked to me and my siblings, apologizing for the violence we witnessed growing up.

Mother let me know the love she had for me and she could not force a man to be a father, but the Heavenly Father/Lord was my father. I did not want to hear that and did not understand what she meant, even though she said it each time I duplicated anger and hurt. I would always tell my mother, that she will never understand the feeling of people saying how I was my father's twin, when he wanted nothing to do with me.

* Miciayah Version

One thing about me is, I don't know why I was so angry, but I was. I did not know how to verbalize my pain. My mother would always talk to me and ask me questions when she sensed something was wrong. I would tell her what I was feeling inside, and she would get upset because there was nothing, she could do about it. She was a good mother and always provided for me beyond the essentials of what I needed as a kid. I even got whatever I wanted, but always said how mom still did not understand.

After years of not going over my father's house wherever he resided, I still saw him at grandma house. He would greet me, often with a hug but never really say anything to me the entire time of the visit. That always made me feel torn up inside, lost and thoughts of why? What did I do? When my father had two other kids and named them similar to my brother and I, I thought WOW!
He was really trying to replace me and my brother. Especially since I was not visiting him like I use to and, he

did not reach out to see how I was doing over time. I tried so many years to block things from my mind and make my mind believe certain events did not occur or that my father really did love me.

My life was like a spiral because at times I was happy and feeling good about school, friends and just having fun as a child. Then the moment I see kids with their fathers or friends talking about their father even if the conversation was not always happy, their father was involved. I would get so angry sometimes, I would run out the classroom and yell at my teacher. Not all of them, just the ones reminding me of something or someone, but they did not understand my anger and frustration. I was a hurt little girl needing her daddy presence in her life. Yes, I still saw him with his new family and another son and daughter, I grew to love and accept. My little sister and brother eventually got to know me and I was always embraced with warmth from his girlfriend.

My father's women were always nice to me and my father always portrayed himself to be the ideal father to them. What use to get me so angered, was when my father would post pictures of me along with himself and sometimes with my brother on social media. He made the world believe that he was this loving, caring and considerate father that takes care of his children. He had the world believing he had a relationship with me, but it was a fallacy. Although, I wish it was true, unfortunately, as of today the disconnect is my reality.

I struggled always thinking what was it keeping my father separated from me. I looked just like him with dark skin, full eyebrows, full lips, and everyone called me his twin and his mother's mini-me. It angered me as years passed with the absence of my father's love; I always blamed myself, I thought I was not pretty or smart enough. It hurt my mother to hear me say that and she would always try to convince me that was not the case; but I did not believe her. I always told my mother she was lighter than me and I was adopted. That was something I was told by bullies in school and I started to believe it, because of the hurt I already endured.

The anger I duplicated was not only my own; but I inherited it. It was given to me by the exposure I had in my youth. It was given to me by my mother. It was given to me by my peers in school. My anger was given to me by my community. My anger was given to me by the void in my heart and I hold my father responsible for creating it and allowing it to flourish inside me.

Chapter 3

The Hurt I Feel

*Ariel Version

Imagine at 15 years old, your father is getting married and you nor your sister did not get invited. But all his other kids including your siblings through another mother, family and friends were there. Then hearing from your big brother how dad stated he didn't like me or my sister's behavior, therefore, he didn't invite us. How hurtful is that? Well, it was very hurtful and another experience to add to all those memories I unconsciously count.

From my infancy into my youth and into young adulthood, sometimes I feel so invisible. The hurt I carry just doesn't seem to go away. I had become a delinquent, got into the streets, and did destructive acts because of my anger. My actions landed me in jail several times and even on home monitoring. I always tell people because they always ask, what am I so hurt about, and I simply tell them; I don't have a dad. My mother over the years has been so apologetic for my father's non-involvement in my life.

Just thinking about my past and all the hurt I went through being fatherless during important events in my life hurts my stomach. The disappointment I felt inside had me hurt and lashing out on anyone I was around that made me upset. I was so hurt at times I questioned my existence. Therefore, I continued to engage in behaviors that kept my mind in a hypnotic state. I did not feel the pain when I was in my hypnotic mindset, instead I became calm and playfully energetic.

Even though I was full of hurt, my mom always tried to instill love within me. My mother always told me how proud of me she was and also demonstrated her frustration and hurt when I did wrong. But my mother never gave up on me. Instead, my mother encouraged me to utilize my hurt and anger constructively. I did just that and started to use my anger and hurt to discover a passion that I now love. Yes, I discovered love. Through years of not having my father involved in my life and feeling unloved, dug holes within my soul.

Once I discovered I love music, those holes slowly started to fill. Even though, I was still lashing out and being hurtful to those who did love me, I was trying it figure it all out. I did not truly get a chance to be the kid, I could have been due to so much pain. I am not saying my childhood was tortuous because it was not, I had a lot of wonderful moments with my family on my mom side. On my dads' side, I did have some memorable moments of laughter and excitement, especially from being my grandma's little Zeebe.

I have learned over the years that hurt and pain does not just go away, it does not vanish on its own. It lays dormant inside until it is activated by my thoughts, or the actions or words of others. It has not been easy to just put the thoughts I carry from the hurt of not being able to talk, to my father as his son in an everlasting resting state. I have tried numerous times, year after year but my hurt will not go away. If I had one wish, I knew would come true, it would be to start over with a father in my life. People judge me all the time, thinking what is wrong with this kid; I have heard it all. The external part of me is well put together, I stay fly. It's the inside of me that has been broken, and as I develop in human form into an adult, I intend to recreate a person who is whole. It takes a lot of therapy, and family support to understand that narrative.

Miciayah Version

I always ask myself, why do I feel the way I do. It's like my emotions and hurt I feel is not my own. I do everything I can to not feel the way I do, which are feelings of sadness, loneliness, and hate. I know hate is a strong word, but I am a kid entitled to express how I feel. The way I know how to release the hurt I have on my surface, is to explode with rage. Of course, I did not think a lot of my actions out when I did things that would come back to resurface in my life. I did try to reason with my hurt and tell it, if it did not hurt me so much, I would be a better person. But there was no compromising with the selfish emotion that has taken over my soul.

I try not to think of moments that hurt me the most. I am one of those people who try to avoid conversation that wakes up the hurt inside I carry. I have tried numerous times to block out certain events and feelings that have sunken within the core of my being. My mother told me I was specially designed by the Lord and everything about me was beautiful. I never believed that because my hurt was so great it was impossible to replace. What hurt me the most is that I carried a trait that was responsible for monthly hospital visits, since I was two and being told I have to take prescriptions for the rest of my life. But what even hurt me greater than that is the fact of my father knowing all of this and still chooses not to be a part of my life.

I am not the kind of kid that wants pity and people feeling sorry for me. I am the kind of kid that wants to feel normal, that wants to be lifted up and encouraged until I can feel empowered. I am the kind of kid that needed a mother and father in my life, even if they were not in a relationship. All the bad stuff my father has done to my mother, she still gave him a chance to be a father to me and he chose to walk away and that hurt me beyond words.

As I grew and learned to develop positive and therapeutic coping skills, it felt like my hurt got stronger because I had to face it. I had to feel the unconscious hurt in me that was four, five or a year old hurt that aroused emotions as if, it was presently occurring. I had to constantly deceive my own mind as if the person I made responsible for my hurt was not my father. I came to a point where I did not want to accept that a man who abandoned me was considered my father. Some people did not understand my pain, frustration and all the intense tension stored inside of me.

I had so many people that did not like something about me for their own reasons. I was told I was too tall, I was too skinny, I was to dark, my eyes were too yellow. I was criticized everyday it seemed like by someone close to me, or the bullies at my school. I became an emotional roller coaster in where, I just did not care about anything at one moment then suddenly, I was sensitive to everything. I have watched movies about girls that felt like I did. I have seen positive and negative outcomes of how those girls grow up to be after such trauma.

I know everyone experiences trauma, and some people do recover to live productive lives. While other people live their whole life unhappy and miserable because of the trauma they endured. My trauma started incredibly young and for an awfully long time, I let the trauma of my father not being in my life almost destroy me. But, through family support from my mom and family, I am learning to accept the thing I cannot change. I have overcome a lot of obstacles in my life and as I still struggle to maintain a balance within me, the hurt I feel is now different.

Chapter 4

Learning to Let Go

*Ariel Version

I am learning to let go of all my pain and hurt through my music. I am able to redirect my anger to the lyrics I write and feel empowered and inspired.

I was just a little boy, I was sitting in the field, I was watching other kids run up and down the hill. Watching kid's dad throw Frisbees' feeling kind of sad. The emptiness inside of me kept me feeling kind of mad. Feeling like I'm in this dark world all alone. Now I'm damn near grown writing million-dollar songs. (Gloski 2020)

There are times, and I don't know why, that I just get angry and upset I don't have a father. I have gotten sidetracked and let my anger along with negative influences throw me off course. My mother has always said, I need to let go, and she was tired of hearing the I don't have a father story. I would get upset when my father, to this day only acknowledges me when it's convenient for him. Situations like if I get into serious trouble and his family is talking about it, then maybe he'll reach out. Or times where he has posted my picture on social media like he's a proud father and showing me off. Or played my music like he helped me to furnish my dreams. After all these years, I still don't have the communication or relationship I want from my father.

On the other hand, my mother believes she has given me father figures, and I was blessed to have men in my life many have opened up to me about their experiences growing up without a father. My mother believes she has provided me with what I needed and beyond to let go of my anger and rage. My mother has been a very influential person in my life who has always been there for me, even at times when I did not deserve her kindness. It was time to let go because if I did not, I would not grow into the man I desire to be.

It is hard letting go especially when I have lived a certain way for so long. When the answers to questions I want my father to answer, I never got to ask. And wondering at this point in my life would I even let go of my ego and be vulnerable enough to do so. I would have preferred for my father to come to me and have a man to man talk but as of now it has not happened. I know he has called me disrespectful with behavior issues but there are always layers behind assumption. When the time was never taken out to get to know the real me. Why can other people see the good in me, but he can't. I strive to let go of all my built-up anger, resentment, and pain. Especially since the world continues to face a global pandemic such as Covid-19. I use this moment in time as my platform to be heard. I use this platform to let go and grow. I use this platform in hope to inspire others to mend father and son's broken relationships.

As I fight through my own demons to be a better son, brother, grandson, cousin, and friend; I am learning to let go. I strive not to let other people's actions negatively affect me because I am blessed with the gift of life. I am here on earth by divine purpose and for the rest of my life I want to make it count. I want my days to be full of happiness. Therefore, I now know that I have a choice to continue to be hurt and sad demonstrating an unbalance within me. I can yearn for artificial affection with words if not actions. Or I can let go of my past, create my future, and embrace myself. I was told by a wise lady once I do all of that then I will discover something great. The something great is, SelfLove! with self-love I am forever with love and I will not need to feel validated by anyone else's love.

**Miciayah Version

I have unintentionally put my mother through so much over the years. I would see my mother crying and feel bad because, I know she loves me, and I was hurting her. I realized my actions not only affect me, but they affected my mother, siblings and those that did care for me as well. I was a growing kid and a teenager that started to see situations in life different, I was maturing, a teenager and soon young adult. I had people that believed in me like my seventh-grade teacher, Mrs. Sommers. She will forever have a place in my heart. Ms. Sommers was one of the reasons I managed to get through all that pain I was going through in school.

It was time for me to stop thinking about my father. I have hoped and prayed so many times over the years my father would change his mind about accepting me in his life as his daughter. All the pain and trauma I have lived through and delinquent behaviors I indulged in was not helping my father to get involved in my life. My mother has always told me that I cannot force anyone to love and except me and that I had to love and accept myself. I never could fully understand what she meant by that but, now as I'm getting older and have experienced some things, I am starting to grasp that concept.

I have had so many people come in and out of my life over the years. I have had some therapist, doctors, fake friends and burned bridges with some family members. I have felt so many different emotions sunken deep into my soul, but I know now is the time I learn to let go. There are so many things I have decided to do in my life when I become an adult and realize I must be mentally and emotionally strong to survive in this world. I have blamed my unhappiness on the absence of my father, and it was time I learn to let go. If I continued to carry years of pain in my heart then, I would never experience love. I know that now and I know the process of transformation comes in stages.

I have never depicted myself to be a perfect child if there was such a thing. All I wanted was a mother and a father that both showed me love as they both engaged in my development. All I ever asked for was to be loved by both parents in a way that showed it through actions of involvement. But now it's time to let go of the little girl who missed all the father and daughter dances. It's time to let go of waiting for something that might never happen. I have to accept certain things in my life and walk in a new direction.

I am not without some hurt and disappointment right now, but I choose not to let it control my life. I decided to choose the path that will lead me to happiness and self-fulfillment. I know that I cannot erase my past of the trauma

I've experienced but I decided to handle my struggles differently. I realized I have a lot of things in my life to be happy and grateful for, therefore I choose to focus on the present and not the past. I have to let go of my father not communicating with me and embrace the love around me. I am not saying if he ever comes to me and wants to establish a relationship that I will push him away. Honestly, I don't know. I would just have to see what my reactions will be if that time ever comes. But I will no longer sit and contemplate on an unknown moment in invisible time.

As of today, I am embracing the rest of my youth. I am enjoying being a teenager and living with my mother and siblings. I am filling my life with memorable moments to cherish. I am recreating my story in life to redirect its course. I am becoming a young lady who is discovering self-love and embracing me. I am freeing myself of the trauma that tried to stay as I am learning to let go.

Chapter 5

A Promise to Myself

*Ariel Version

I have come a long way in my life. I have held on to so many things that kept me in a place in where I could not progress in my life. I probably would have been further in life by now if I would have let go of all that hurt, I had been carrying inside. I might have been more focused on my studies and graduated by now, but I let things take control of me. It is true in life there are many lessons to be learned and if a person wants to grow, then they must understand what was intended, behind a trauma they experienced. I made up so many excuses and put my mother through so much hardship with my actions. It is time for me to stop all the childish behavior and be the young man many look for me to be, because he is within me.

I promise myself from now on, I will be a person of positive energy adding substance and integrity to my character. I will not let what is going on in this chaotic world put fear in me. Even though, so many blacks are dying at the hands of injustice, I pray I never be a statistic. Yes, I am afraid to walk around in the color of my skin with all the strikes against me as a young black man. But the hardest thing I had to endure in my life right now was holding on to the hurt and pain of not having my father in my life. So now, I have freed myself from letting that control my mind, I believe I am full of greatness with gifted talents to bless the world with. I have to make my life matter because if I don't then, no one will. I don't want anything to happen to me and my life for people to say I matter then. I matter now, and I promise to love myself and make my life of greatness.

Miciayah Version

It took me awhile to realize how blessed I am, but over time and through heartache I had an epiphany. I had endured so much during my years on earth, and I thought I would not make it pass a certain age. So many people put negative things in my path and filled my mind with fear and hopelessness that led me to take on that mindset. I also had people try to instill love, warmth, and peace within me. I slowly grew into that mental concept. My mother has told me how powerful my thoughts are and that I have great power within myself to be anything I want to in life. I finally got it! I have not mastered the concept yet because, of course I am young and still have a teenage mind, but I am aware and knowledgeable about the possibilities of my inner self. I now believe in myself and had to learn how to let my past traumas go. Sometimes things pop in my mind and try to hinder and hurt me all over again but, I now realize the power I possess. I have finally accepted my father the way he is and has been and that he might never change but I am ok with it. I have so many other things to focus on now in life.

I promise myself to be a great young woman who is full of life, and positive energy. I know I must continue practicing how to overcome obstacles and not let it take my power away. I believe because I am aware of what trauma does to people, I can now use it as strength. My life from here on out will be amazing because I will make it that way. I am happy and blessed to have my mom and grateful for her wisdom. I promise to not only make my mom proud of me but to make me proud of myself.

POEM

And You Wonder Why

When I sit in silence and scream leave me alone,
I'm thinking about a time that is not yet gone.
When a laughter turns into tears,
I have revisited unsilenced fears.
When I tremble on a warm summer day,
My father above delivered me from prey.
When my mind won't let go of a certain thought,
My heart battles through the trenches I fought.

And you wonder why

When my skin won't let me breathe,
And the depression will not leave.
The pain that seems to never heal,
But they say the cure is in a pill.
Just know that the cure of the broken can be repaired,
Learning not to give my power to those who faked they cared.

And You Wonder Why

And you wonder why, thinking I shamed your name,
It's not about you but for me to recover from internal pain.
I promise myself to forgive me for unconscious blame,
And love the beauty in and out of me that glows through the rain.
To embrace the qualities of my greatness that I slowly discover.
Leaving the life of my youth behind and creating another.

And You Wonder Why

This was necessary to begin a new chapter, so I had to speak,
If you heard me or hear me, self-love is what I seek. Now you know why my trauma once kept me trapped with rage,
That final chapter has ended with this book and its concluded page.
I am my own being that if full of life that I yearn to discover.
Blessed to have my family and strength like my mother.

By: A Face Without Shame (2020)

www.ingramcontent.com/pod-product-compliance
Lightning Source LLC
Chambersburg PA
CBHW051714090426
42736CB00013B/2697